POWER SNACKS

by Kate Schumann and Jennifer Raymond

Introduction by Neal D.Barnard, M.D.

The Magni Group
McKinney, TX

Published by the Magni Group
        P.O. Box 849
        McKinney, TX 75070

Printed in the U.S.A.
ISBN 1-882330-49-8

POWER SNACKS

Snacking does not have to mean gaining weight. With practical tips and delicious recipes, including sweets, savories, and beverages, <u>Power Snacks</u> lets you say "yes" to your taste buds and still lose weight. Using the incredible negative calorie effect, these snacks contain nutrients that help keep your metabolism burning calories faster for hours.

CONTENTS

INTRODUCTION

by Neal D. Barnard, M.D.

You have been really good to yourself--eating exactly right, taking advantage of the foods that melt away the pounds. You can almost feel the weight dissolving away. And you have the confidence of knowing that success at permanent weight control is finally within your reach.

Then one night you make a trip to the kitchen and open the cupboard. To your horror, it is filled with chocolate donuts, potato chips, and cheesy snacks staring at you menacingly.

You slam the cupboard door closed. "No way," you think to yourself. "I'm not going to destroy all my progress with that junk food." You turn to the refrigerator. And there, sliced bologna, cheese, and frozen pizza lie in wait for their next victim. You suddenly feel success slipping through your fingers like sticky melted ice cream.

What is a late-night snacker to do--yield to temptation, knowing you'll regret it later, or say no and go to bed hungry?

When I was in college, my friends and I often made late-night raids on the local "greasy spoon" café for monster burgers and onion rings, all dripping in grease. And we have all found ourselves opening up a packet of cookies and eating far more than we wish we had, or polishing off a carton of ice cream, or maybe throwing aside any semblance of delicacy and just tucking into a big jar of peanut butter with a spoon. More often than we'd like, we have been taken a bit too far by our taste buds, making our waistlines pay the price.

There is a solution. When you have the right kind of snacks on hand, you can kiss those fatty varieties good-bye, along with the pounds they would bring.

This book presents simple recipes that let you treat yourself to all kinds of wonderful snacks, including cakes, pies, and cookies that are delicious, but totally healthy and in synch with your weight-control program. If your taste calls for pizza, dips, or french fries, you'll find easy ways to make them that actually help you lose weight, because they help you burn calories, just as the recipes do in Foods That

6

Cause You to Lose Weight.

Before turning to the recipes, let me share with you a few thoughts about snacking.

First of all, don't be afraid of snacking. The old-fashioned frowning on between-meal snacks has been replaced by the recognition that more frequent meals or snacks can actually be beneficial in some ways, compared to fewer, bigger meals. If, on the other hand, you are intentionally eating small meals to try to lose weight only to need snacks later to deal with the inevitable hunger, go ahead and have more generous meals.

When it comes to snacking, there seems to be a gender difference in the kinds of foods we are drawn to. Women often go for sweets, particularly chocolate, while men tend to seek out fried or salty items, such as potato chips, peanuts, or onion rings, although some men do like sweets and some women prefer savories. It helps to know your tendencies and vulnerabilities, so you can be sure to have healthy varieties of your kind of snack on hand.

If you are drawn to sweets, you'll be glad to know that sugar, used in modest amounts, is not usually the cause of weight problems. It actually has only four calories per gram (a gram is about 1/28th of an ounce). Compare that to the shortening or butter in a typical cookie or cake. Any kind of fat, whether it comes in butter, shortening, margarine, vegetable oil, or any other variety, has nine calories in every gram, more than twice the calories of sugar.

Where sugar does its dirty work is when it acts as a Trojan horse for fat. Sugar lures you in to cakes, cookies, and pies, but it is the butter or shortening baked into them that will expand your waistline.

Of course, if you eat a heroic amount of sugar day after day, you are likely to gain weight. But the point is that the fats and oils in foods are much more likely to cause weight problems than whatever sugar they may contain.

Nature has always offered us sweet snacks that are as healthy as they are delicious. You can't beat fruits for good nutrition, and even though they are naturally sweet, it is almost impossible to gain weight from them. Open up a big, ripe orange. Or bite into a crisp, fresh apple. Enjoy pears, cherries, pineapples, grapefruit, mangoes--you name it.

If you cut a pineapple or watermelon into chunks and put it in the refrigerator on Sunday, you will be delighted to see it on Monday when you get home from work. Or, for convenience, pick up some fruit cocktail or fruit salad at the grocery store.

Fresh fruit is also a handy thing to have in your desk drawer at work, and dried fruit makes a good snack, whether it is the mixed variety sold in vending machines and gift shops, dried apricots, raisins, or whatever.

Speaking of snacking at work, you might also try the new instant soups, which come in a wide variety of flavors. You'll also find couscous, chili, and bean and rice dishes in the same instant cup package. With some rice cakes or low-fat crackers, you've got a hearty snack or even a complete meal, which you can follow with an apple or orange for dessert.

Some commercial products are worth mentioning. Health food stores and kosher groceries carry <u>Tofutti</u>, which has the taste and texture of the finest ice cream, but is made from soy, so it contains no animal fat, animal protein, or lactose sugar. Look for the "lite" varieties. Health food stores carry many other ice cream and yogurt substitutes made from soy or rice, and they are a big improvement over the cow's milk varieties. Read the labels and choose the lowest-fat brands.

Health food stores also offer new varieties of potato chips and tortilla chips. Typical potato chips are made by dropping potato slices into a fryer. As the hot oil soaks in, their calorie content triples. Several companies now offer potato chips that are baked, not fried, so no oil is added. The same goes for tortilla chips, and as you dip them into salsa or bean dip, you'll never know the difference.

While you're at the health food store, take a look at fat-free cookies. You'll also find many varieties of meatless hot dogs, burgers, and deli slices. Read the labels to pick the lowest-fat brands, but they all beat the socks off the meat varieties. You may want to keep some in your fridge for when you get a serious snacking urge.

Grains work their way into healthy snacks, too. A piece of toast or some noodle soup provides plenty of fat-burning complex carbohydrates. Two important tips: don't put butter or margarine on your toast. Top it with jam or cinnamon instead. And go for whole grains which retain the natural fiber. That means whole grain bread or pasta, brown rice, etc.

We don't usually think of popcorn as health food, but it really is a healthy, natural grain. And when it is air-popped, no fat is added. The danger comes if you drip butter all over the top, and the popcorn simply becomes a vehicle for grease that will fatten you up.

If you have a little extra time on a weekend, you may want to make a snack for the following week--a cake, a pie, or some cookies. This is only for those who know they will be snacking and want a healthier version. Don't bother if you would not normally look for a snack.

Which brings me to another important point: Although the foods in this book are just about the healthiest snacks around, the idea is not to gorge yourself, shoveling in one great snack after another. Listen to your natural hunger and satiety cues. If you are hungry, that is a time to eat. When you are full, that is a time to do something else. If you are eating simply because you have nothing else to do, all the snacks in the world will not provide the answer you really need. It is time to explore intellectual or physical "nourishment," if you will--the company of friends, good books, films, sports, games, dancing, or whatever. Don't let food take the place of other parts of life.

Many of our between-meal trips to the refrigerator or the store are for beverages rather than food, so let's talk for a minute about these pourable snacks.

The fact is, as far as beverages go, all the body really needs is water, and it is a lot healthier than sodas. Sodas contain either sugar or artificial sweeteners, neither of which your body really needs. NutraSweet, in particular, has been the subject of scientific reports linking it to headaches, behavioral disturbances, and even grand mal seizures. While the toxicologists try to sort out whether it is safe or not, it is worth noting that NutraSweet has been no magic wand for weight problems.

But compared to cola commercials showing teenagers partying on the beach, a glass of water seems pretty dull. Luckily, water has taken on a new sophisticated image, thanks to Evian and Perrier. After all, what cola comes from underground springs in the French Alps? To dress it up, use a squirt of juice from a freshly cut lemon or lime. If you like a thick, sweet shake, try the recipes for fruit smoothies. Kids love them, and you will, too.

If your idea of a healthy beverage is a jolt of caffeine, you will be glad to know that one or two cups of coffee per day does not have serious health consequences, so far as anyone knows, although caffeine can make premenstrual syndrome worse, and if you have more than two cups per day, the caffeine will encourage the loss of calcium from your bones.

Speaking of health concerns, you may have already been paying close attention to the kinds of snacks you eat because of their effect on your cholesterol level, for example. You will be glad to know that all the snacks in this book have no cholesterol at all and tend to be low in fat.

If you have diabetes, you already know that sugary snacks can make it hard to manage your blood sugar, but are necessary when your blood sugar gets too low. You will find that avoiding fatty snacks helps, too, since reducing fat intake helps insulin to work better. Also, snacks made from beans and other legumes often have less effect on blood sugar than other foods. Try white bean dip with fresh ginger and lime, hummus, or bean burritos, or open a can of lentil soup. Whole foods, such as brown rice or whole grain breads are better than refined foods, such as white rice or white bread.

If you have high blood pressure, you have probably been shying away from salty snacks, like potato chips and pretzels, and for good reason. Salt can increase your blood pressure. But it is just as important-- maybe even more important--to avoid fatty snacks. When people go on very-low-fat diets, especially vegetarian diets, their blood pressure tends to drop. So don't have chicken salad or beef jerky as your appetite-quencher. Have the healthy, low-fat snacks you'll see in this book.

I hope you enjoy these healthy power snacks.

WHITE BEAN DIP WITH FRESH GINGER AND LIME

Minced ginger and fresh lime add a sparkling freshness to this low-fat bean dip. It is delicious with raw vegetables, crackers, or as a spread for crusty whole wheat bread.

3 Cups Cooked White, Navy, Or Cannellini Beans, Or 2 Cans Drained Rinsed Beans
1 Tablespoon Olive Oil (Optional)
Zest And Juice Of 1 Lime (Scrape Off The Zest Before You Squeeze The Juice)
2 Or 3 Garlic Cloves, Peeled And Minced Or Pressed Through A Garlic Press
1 1-Inch Piece Fresh Ginger Root, Peeled And Minced
2 To 3 Green Onions, Minced, Including Some Green Tops
Dash Of Hot Sauce
1/4 Teaspoon Salt (Optional)
3 Tablespoons Chopped Cilantro

In a blender or food processor, process the beans, olive oil, lime zest and juice, garlic, minced ginger, green onion, hot sauce, and salt until smooth. Transfer to a medium bowl and add chopped cilantro. Serve either chilled or at room temperature.

Serves 6

PITA PIZZAS

Pita bread makes a terrific crust for quick and easy individual pizzas that you can make in a regular oven or a toaster oven. You can use a commercial pizza sauce or make your own with the following recipe.

1 15-ounce can tomato sauce
1 6-ounce can tomato paste
1 teaspoon each: garlic powder and dried basil
1/2 teaspoon each: dried oregano and thyme
6 pita breads
2 cups chopped vegetables: green onion, bell pepper, mushrooms, and/or olives

Preheat the broiler.
Combine tomato sauce, tomato paste, and seasonings. This will make about twice as much sauce as you need. The extra may be refrigerated or frozen for future use.

To assemble the pizza, turn pita bread upside down so it looks like a saucer. Spread with tomato sauce, then top liberally with chopped vegetables. Place on a cookie sheet and broil about 5 minutes, or until the edges just start to get crisp. Or place individual pizzas in toaster oven and toast for 3 to 5 minutes.

Makes 6 Pizzas

HUMMUS

Hummus (pronounced HUMM-us) is a delicious Middle-Eastern chickpea pâté served with crackers, wedges of pita bread, or fresh vegetable slices. It also makes a delicious sandwich spread. It is easy to make in a food processor--just add all the ingredients and process until smooth--or by hand. Store it in an airtight container in the refrigerator for up to a week for quick sandwiches and snacks.

2 cups cooked chickpeas, or 1 15-ounce can
1-2 garlic cloves, minced
1/4 cup tahini (sesame seed butter)
2 tablespoons lemon juice

1/4 teaspoon salt
1 tablespoon finely chopped fresh parsley
1/4 teaspoon each: ground cumin and paprika

Drain the chickpeas, reserving the liquid. Mash the beans, then add the remaining ingredients and mix well. The texture should be creamy and spreadable. If it is too dry, add enough of the reserved bean liquid to achieve the desired consistency. For a fat-free version, replace the tahini with 1 finely grated carrot.

Serves 6 To 8

WHOLE WHEAT HERBED PITA CHIPS

Separate medium-sized whole wheat pita bread into halves. Then cut each half into eighths. Arrange on a cookie sheet, spray lightly with olive oil Pam and dust with garlic salt and mixed crushed dried herbs. Thyme and oregano make an especially good combination.

WHOLE WHEAT CRACKERS WITH CINNAMON SUGAR

Look for Ak-Mak whole-wheat crackers at the grocery store. They are delicious whole-wheat, non-fat crackers that are great with dips. They can also satisfy a sweet-tooth. Place them on a cookie sheet, spray lightly with Pam or other light oil spray, and dust with cinnamon sugar. Bake at 350 degrees F. for 5 minutes. This recipe also works with Ry Krisp or any similar cracker.

WHOLE WHEAT CRACKERS WITH HERBS

Follow above directions, but spray with an olive oil spray and lightly dust on your favorite Italian herb blend and a dash of garlic salt.

QUICK BLACK BEAN DIP WITH CORN TORTILLA CHIPS

Fantastic Foods makes a delicious Black Bean Dip that you'll find at most groceries and at all health food stores. Just follow the directions on the box.

You will also find no-fat, baked tortilla chips at health food stores. Or try this easy way of making your own: Cut a stack of tortillas into eighths and toast the wedges on an ungreased cookie sheet until lightly tanned. Watch carefully--they seem to brown just when you look the other way. For added flavor, give them a quick spray with Pam and sprinkle on an herb and spice blend seasoning. McCormick makes a spicy salt-free Popcorn Blend that is particularly good with "South-of the-Border" food.

QUICK VEGETABLE RAMEN

You'll find ramen soups in many different flavors at health foods stores and most supermarkets. The package contains dried noodles that cook in 2 to 3 minutes and a packet of flavorful seasoning broth. By adding your own fresh vegetables, you can dress ramen noodles up a bit, and make a tasty, nutritious snack or meal.

1 package ramen soup
1 cup chopped broccoli
1 green onion, sliced

Follow the package instructions for cooking ramen. Add the broccoli to the boiling water along with the noodles. Stir in the sliced green onion just before serving.

Serves 2

CARROT AND RAISIN SALAD

This is a great snacking salad that will stay fresh and crisp for several days if tightly covered and refrigerated. Grate the carrots and toss with remaining ingredients. Hold the sunflower seeds until just ready to serve, and go lightly, as they do contain fat.

1 1/2 lb carrots
2 teaspoons canola oil
Juice from 1 large lemon
1 tablespoon raspberry vinegar
1/2 cup raisins
1 tablespoon roasted sunflower seeds (optional)

Serves 6

FOUR BEAN SALAD

This quick salad keeps well in the refrigerator for a tasty snack.

1 15-ounce can dark kidney beans, drained
1 15-ounce can black-eyed peas, drained
1 10-ounce package frozen lima beans, thawed
1 15-ounce can S & W Pinquitos or other vegetarian chili beans
1 large red bell pepper, diced
1/2 cup finely chopped onion
2 cups fresh or frozen corn
1/4 cup seasoned rice vinegar
2 tablespoons apple cider or distilled vinegar
1 lemon, juiced
2 teaspoons cumin
1 teaspoon coriander
1/8 teaspoon cayenne

Drain the kidney beans, black-eyed peas, and lima beans and combine in a large bowl. Add the pinquitos or chili beans along with their sauce. Stir in the bell pepper, onion, and corn.

Whisk the remaining ingredients together and pour over the salad. Toss gently to mix. Chill at least 1 hour before serving, if possible.

Serves 10

MOCK TUNA SALAD

This is amazingly fast way to whip up a healthy sandwich spread, and it has none of the fat, mercury, or other undesirables found in tuna fish.

1 15-ounce can chickpeas, drained
1 stalk celery, finely chopped
1 medium carrot, grated (optional)
1 green onion, finely chopped
2 teaspoons Dijon mustard or eggless mayonnaise
1 tablespoon sweet pickle relish
1/4 teaspoon salt (optional)

Mash the chickpeas with a fork or potato masher. Leave some chunks. Add the celery, carrot, green onion, mayonnaise, and relish. Add salt to taste.

Serve on whole wheat bread or in pita bread with lettuce and sliced tomatoes.

Makes 4 Sandwiches

EGGLESS SALAD SANDWICH

Do you love egg salad, but hate the fat and cholesterol? Here's a better way.

1/2 pound firm tofu, mashed
1 green onion, finely chopped
2 tablespoons eggless mayonnaise
1 tablespoon pickle relish
1 teaspoon mustard
1/4 teaspoon each: ground cumin, turmeric, and garlic powder
Pinch of salt

Combine all ingredients and mix thoroughly. Serve on whole wheat bread with lettuce and tomato.

Makes 4 Sandwiches

BEAN BURRITO WITH SALSA

A burrito makes a great snack or a quick meal. By the way, the term "refried beans" is really a misnomer. They are boiled, and fat-free and vegetarian varieties are widely available.

1 15-ounce can refried beans
1 16-ounce jar salsa
1 package whole wheat tortillas

Heat the beans in one pan and the salsa in another. Heat a tortilla in a dry, heavy skillet over moderate heat until it is warm and flexible. Remove from pan and spread refried beans in a line down the middle of the tortilla. Fold in the ends, then starting at one side, roll up around the beans. Place on a plate, then spoon heated salsa over the top.

Makes 6 Burritos

QUICKIE QUESADILLAS

These quesadillas are made with Cheezy Garbanzo Spread. If you make the spread in advance, the quesadillas can be prepared in a jiffy.

1 recipe Cheezy Garbanzo Spread (recipe follows)
12 corn tortillas
3 to 4 green onions, sliced
1 bell pepper, seeded and diced (optional)
2 cups diced tomatoes (optional)
1 cup salsa

Spread 2 to 3 tablespoons of the garbanzo spread on a tortilla and place it, spread side up, in a large heated skillet. As soon as it is warm and soft, fold it in half, then cook it another minute. Remove it from the pan and carefully open it. Sprinkle on some green onions, bell pepper, tomatoes, and salsa. Repeat with the remaining tortillas.

Makes 12 quesadillas, 6 servings

CHEEZY GARBANZO SPREAD

Try this spread on bread and crackers, or in the quesadilla recipe above. Look for jars of water-packed roasted red peppers near the pickles and olives in your grocery store. Tahini is available in most supermarkets and health food stores.

1 15-ounce can garbanzo beans
1/2 cup roasted red peppers
3 tablespoons tahini (sesame seed butter)
3 tablespoons lemon juice

Drain the garbanzo beans, reserving the liquid, and place them in a food processor or blender with the remaining ingredients. Process until very smooth. If using a blender, you will have to stop it occasionally and push everything down into the blades with a rubber spatula. The mixture should be quite thick, but if it is too thick to blend, add a tablespoon or two of the reserved bean liquid.

Makes about 2 cups, 8 1/4-cup servings

ROASTED GARLIC AND GARLIC BREAD

This is a delight for serious snackers. Roasting brings out garlic's milder side. Start with a large, firm head of garlic. Place it into a small baking dish. Bake in a toaster oven or a regular oven at 375 degrees F. until the cloves feel soft when pressed lightly, about 25 minutes.

Then, just pick off a clove and pop it in your mouth. Or use it as a spread for bread. You can store it in the refrigerator for up to two weeks.

To make garlic bread, use a fork to mash peeled cloves of roasted garlic into a paste. Spread with a knife onto slices of French bread. Sprinkle with Italian seasoning if desired. Wrap tightly in foil and bake at 350 degrees F. for 20 minutes.

OVEN "FRIED" POTATOES

3 pounds medium baking potatoes
1 tablespoon vegetable oil
1 to 2 teaspoons chili powder

Preheat the oven to 425 degrees F. Coat a large rimmed baking pan with vegetable cooking spray. Cut each potato in half lengthwise, then cut each half lengthwise into quarters. In a large bowl, toss together potatoes, oil, and chili powder until the potato wedges are well coated. Spread potatoes on a greased pan in one layer. Bake for about 20 minutes, or until nicely browned.

Serves 8

JICAMA WITH ORANGE JUICE AND MINT

Jicama, a crisp, mild-tasting root, takes on the flavor of whatever it is with. Peel it and cut it in thin slices. Arrange in a bowl and pour over fresh squeezed orange juice and fresh or dried chopped mint leaves. Toss ingredients and refrigerate for several hours.

JICAMA WITH LIME JUICE AND MEXICAN SEASONING

Peel and slice the jicama into long narrow pieces about 1/4 inch thick by 1/2 inch wide. Arrange on a flat pan and sprinkle the slices with fresh lime juice and Mexican Seasoning or a mixture of garlic salt and chili powder. Refrigerate at least 1/2 hour.

CARAMEL CORN

Here is an easy Cracker Jack-like snack. Use the greater amount of popcorn if you prefer a less sweet snack.

3/4 cup packed brown sugar
4 tablespoons margarine
3 tablespoons corn syrup or other liquid sweetener
1/4 teaspoon salt
1/4 teaspoon baking soda
1/4 teaspoon vanilla extract
8 to 12 cups popped popcorn
1 cup peanuts (optional)

Combine the sugar, margarine, corn syrup, and salt in a saucepan and cook over low heat until the margarine is melted. Then continue to cook (without stirring) for 3 minutes. Add the baking soda and vanilla. Pour over popcorn and peanuts and mix until evenly coated. Bake for 15 minutes at 300 degrees F. Break into pieces.

GINGERBREAD CAKE

This quick and delightful recipe comes from Mary Clifford, a wonderful cook. A dab of peanut butter adds a rich but mellow flavor to an old-time favorite. Let this cake cool completely before slicing or it will be crumbly.

1/3 cup margarine
1/3 cup firmly packed dark brown sugar
1 1/2 tablespoons peanut butter
3/4 cup light molasses
2 cups unsifted all-purpose flour
1 tablespoon baking powder
1 tablespoon ground ginger
1 teaspoon cinnamon
1/2 teaspoon ground nutmeg
Pinch of salt
3/4 cup water

Preheat the oven to 325 degrees. Grease and flour an 8-inch round cake pan.

In a large bowl, cream together the margarine, brown sugar, peanut butter, molasses. Mix together flour, baking powder, ginger, cinnamon, nutmeg and salt and stir into margarine mixture alternately with water until well combined. Pour batter into prepared pan. Bake about 40 minutes, or until cake tester or knife inserted in center comes out clean. Let cool completely on a wire rack.

Serves 8

CARROT CAKE

This delicious cake is also wonderfully healthy--only 9% of its calories come from fat, even with the frosting, and no cholesterol at all.

2 cups grated carrots
1 1/2 cups raisins
2 cups water
1 1/2 teaspoons cinnamon
1 1/2 teaspoons allspice
1/2 teaspoon cloves
1 cup sugar
1/2 teaspoon salt
3 cups unbleached or whole wheat pastry flour
1 1/2 teaspoons baking soda
1 cup soy milk
Tofu Cream Frosting (see below)

Simmer the grated carrots, raisins, water, and spices in a saucepan for 10 minutes. Stir in the sugar and salt and simmer for 2 more minutes. Cool completely. Preheat the oven to 350 degrees F.

In a large bowl, stir the flour and soda together. Add the cooled carrot mixture along with the soy milk and stir just to mix. Spray a 9 x 9-inch pan with nonstick spray and spread the batter in it. Bake for 1 hour. A toothpick inserted into the center should come out clean. Serve plain or frost when completely cooled.

Serves 9

TOFU CREAM FROSTING

1 cup firm tofu (1/2 pound)
2 tablespoons oil
2 tablespoons fresh lemon juice
3 to 4 tablespoons maple syrup
1/4 teaspoon salt
1/2 teaspoon vanilla extract

Combine all the ingredients in a blender and blend until very smooth. Scrape the sides of blender often with a rubber spatula to get the frosting completely smooth.

Makes 1 1/3 cups, enough to frost a 9 x 9-inch cake

BANANA CAKE

2 cups unbleached all-purpose or whole wheat pastry flour
1 1/2 teaspoons baking soda
1/2 teaspoon salt
1 cup raw sugar or other sweetener
1/3 cup oil
4 ripe bananas, mashed (about 2 1/2 cups)
1/4 cup water
1 teaspoon vanilla extract
1 cup chopped walnuts

Preheat the oven to 350 degrees F.

Mix flour, baking soda, and salt in a bowl. In a large bowl, beat sugar and oil together, then add the bananas and mash them. Stir in the water and vanilla, and mix thoroughly. Add the flour mixture along with the chopped walnuts, and stir to mix.

Spread in a nonstick or lightly oil-sprayed 9-inch square baking pan, and bake for 45 to 50 minutes, or until a toothpick inserted into the center comes out clean.

Serves 8

PUMPKIN PIE

This unique recipe uses creamy, blended tofu instead of eggs and milk for a pie that is less fatty and is especially rich tasting.

1 16-ounce can pumpkin
1 teaspoon cinnamon
1/2 teaspoon ginger
1/4 teaspoon nutmeg
1/8 teaspoon ground cloves
1/2 teaspoon salt
1 teaspoon vanilla extract
1 cup light brown sugar
1 tablespoon molasses
3/4 pound soft tofu
1 unbaked pie shell

Preheat the oven to 350 degrees. Combine all ingredients except tofu and pie shell in a blender and blend until mixed and completely smooth. Break the tofu into chunks and add to the pumpkin mixture. Blend well. Pour the filling into the pie shell. Bake for 1 hour. Chill completely before serving.

Serves 8

PUMPKIN SPICE COOKIES

These plump, moist cookies are an unusual treat. They use flaxseeds as a binder, rather than eggs. Flaxseeds are found at any health food store.

3 cups whole wheat pastry flour
4 teaspoons baking powder
1 teaspoon salt
1 teaspoon baking soda
1 teaspoon ground cinnamon
1/2 teaspoon grated nutmeg
1 1/2 cups raw sugar or other sweetener
4 tablespoons flaxseeds
1 1/2 cups water
1 3/4 cups sold-pack canned pumpkin
1 cup raisins

Preheat the oven to 350 degrees F.

Mix the dry ingredients and set aside.

Blend flaxseeds and 1 cup water in a blender for 1 to 2 minutes, until the mixture has the consistency of beaten egg white. Add to the dry ingredients, along with the pumpkin, remaining water, and raisins. Mix until just combined.

Drop by tablespoonfuls onto a nonstick or lightly oil-sprayed baking sheet. Bake 15 minutes, or until lightly browned. Remove from baking sheet with a spatula, and place on a rack to cool. Store in an airtight container.

Makes 3 Dozen Cookies

OLD-FASHIONED OATMEAL COOKIES

1/4 pound margarine
1/2 cup firmly packed brown sugar
1/4 cup sugar
1 tablespoon soy flour
1/2 teaspoon vanilla extract
3/4 cup unbleached flour
1/2 teaspoon baking soda
1/2 teaspoon cinnamon
1 1/2 cups rolled oats (or quick oats)
1/2 cup raisins

Preheat the oven to 350 degrees. Beat together the margarine and sugars until creamy. Add the soy flour and water and beat well to blend.

In a separate bowl, combine the flour, baking soda, and cinnamon. Add to the margarine mixture and mix completely. Stir in the oats and raisins.

Drop by rounded teaspoonfuls onto ungreased cookie sheets. Bake for 10 to 12 minutes, or until light golden brown.

Makes 24 Cookies

GINGERED MELON WEDGES

Use cantaloupe or any other favorite melon for this recipe, which is a fast and elegant dessert.

1 large cantaloupe
1 scant tablespoon powdered sugar
1/2 teaspoon ground ginger
1 tablespoon candied ginger (optional)

Cut melon in half and seed. Then cut each half into chunks. Stir together the sugar and ground ginger. Add candied ginger if you like. Sprinkle over melon chunks and chill.

Serves 6

MIMOSA GRANITA

A refreshing, non-fat Italian ice.

1 cup juice from 3 medium oranges
1/2 cup sugar
1 1/4 cup sparkling apple juice or other sparkling fruit juice
1 tablespoon lime juice

Whisk orange juice and sugar in large bowl until sugar dissolves. Stir in sparkling juice and lime juice and pour mixture into 2 ice cube trays.

Freeze mixture until firm, at least 2 hours. If you like, you can keep frozen cubes in zipper-lock plastic bags up to 1 week. Just before serving, place a single layer of frozen cubes in the bowl of a food processor fitted with a steel blade. Pulse 10 or 12 times or until no large chunks of ice remain. Scoop crystals into individual bowls. Repeat with remaining ice cubes and serve immediately.

Serves 4

KIWI SORBET

An icy treat for the hottest summer days.

4 kiwi
One 6-ounce can lemonade concentrate, thawed
2 cups water

Peel the kiwi and process in blender or food processor just until smooth. (Do not crush the seeds.) Stir in lemonade concentrate and water. Pour mixture into a metal pan. Cover with foil and freeze until firm.

Remove from freezer and let stand 10 minutes. Break into small pieces and put into food processor. Process until smooth. Pack into a plastic container and cover. Return to freezer until firm. Serve by scooping.

Serves 8

TROPICAL DELIGHT

Puréed frozen fruit makes a wonderful snack or dessert. To freeze bananas, peel and break into chunks. Freeze in a single layer on a tray, then store in an airtight container. You will find frozen pineapple and mango at the grocery store, or you can make your own by freezing canned pineapple chunks and fresh mango.

1 orange, peeled
1/2 cup frozen banana chunks
1 cup frozen pineapple chunks
1 cup frozen mango chunks
1/2 to 1 cup soy milk

Cut the orange in half and remove any seeds, then place in a blender with the remaining ingredients and process until thick and very smooth.

Serves 3

STRAWBERRY FREEZE

1 cup frozen strawberries
1 cup frozen banana chunks
1/2 cup unsweetened apple juice

Place all ingredients into blender and process on high speed until thick and smooth. You will have to stop the blender frequently and stir the unblended fruit to the center.

Serves 2

BANANA FREEZE

1/2 cup soymilk or rice milk
1 cup frozen banana chunks

Place soymilk and banana in blender and blend until thick and smooth, stopping the blender occasionally to stir the unblended fruit to the center.

For a delicious variation, add 3 pitted dates to the banana and soymilk, and process as above.

Serves 1

FRUIT POPSICLES

A fun and easy-to-make treat.

1 ripe banana, peeled
1 ripe peach, peeled
6 to 8 strawberries, hulled
1 tablespoon brown sugar
1/4 cup soy milk
1/4 cup fruit juice (apricot nectar, orange juice, white grape juice, or other juice of your choice)

Put all ingredients in a blender and process until smooth. Pour into small paper cups and place on a tray in the freezer. Add popsicle sticks when the mixture has thickened slightly. Continue to freeze until firm.

Serves 4

STRAWBERRY SMOOTHIE

Here is a thick and creamy shake that's a great, quick, and easy way to start your morning or a refreshing way to cool off on a hot summer's day. It's always a hit with kids, too.

1 frozen banana, cut into chunks (peel and wrap banana in plastic wrap before putting in freezer)
1/2 cup frozen strawberries or a mixture of berries and other fruit
1/2 cup vanilla soymilk
2 tablespoons strawberry or other fruit syrup
3 ice cubes

Place all ingredients in a blender and blend on high speed until smooth and creamy.

Serves 2

MINTY RED ZINGER ICED TEA

2 to 3 tea bags of Red Zinger or other robust herb tea
1/2 to 1 cup of fresh mint leaves (stems and all)
1 tablespoon sugar or liquid sweetener
6 cups boiling water

Place tea bags, mint leaves, and sugar in a large tea pot or pitcher, and pour in 6 cups boiling water. Let steep at least one hour, then cool in refrigerator before adding ice.

PEACH-FLAVORED HERB ICED TEA

Follow the above directions, substituting your favorite herbed tea blend, 2 cardamom pods, a stick of cinnamon and a sliced peach. Steep well before chilling. Strain and serve iced with a sprig of lemon balm or mint.

GREEN TEA COOLER

2-inch piece of fresh ginger root, cut into quarters
4 bags green tea
1 tablespoon sugar
4 cups of boiling water
1 bottle ginger ale

Place ginger, tea bags and sugar in a pitcher. Pour over 4 cups of boiling water. Let steep at least 30 minutes and cool before adding ginger ale. You can make up this "base" and keep in the refrigerator. When ready to serve, add ginger ale (half tea mixture and half ginger ale is a good mixture) and serve with ice and a sprig of mint.

POWER SNACKING TIPS

● Snacking can be a healthy part of your weight control program. The healthiest snacks are very low in fat and get most of their calories from carbohydrates.

● Fruits, including dried fruits, are a terrific snack anytime.

● Sugar is less of a problem than fats in foods. But when sugar lures you to cookies or cakes, the fat they hold really can be fattening.

● The best snacks omit animal products and keep vegetable oils to a bare minimum.

● Snacks made from whole grains, such as whole-grain toast, are preferable to refined grains, which have the fiber removed.

● Your natural hunger and satiety cues will help you. Even though the snacks in this book are great for keeping the pounds off, there is no value in continuing to eat when you are no longer hungry.

● New products at health food stores make snacking easier and healthier than ever: instant soups, healthy desserts, meatless deli slices, potato chips and tortilla chips that are baked, rather than fried, etc.

● There is no need for diet sodas. The only beverage your body really needs is water, in any of the many forms it comes. Add a twist of lemon for a satisfying thirst-quencher.